ILLUSTRATED BIOGRAPHY FOR KIDS

MARIE CURIE

EXTRAORDINARY SCIENTIST

WHO CHANGED THE WORLD

Wonder House

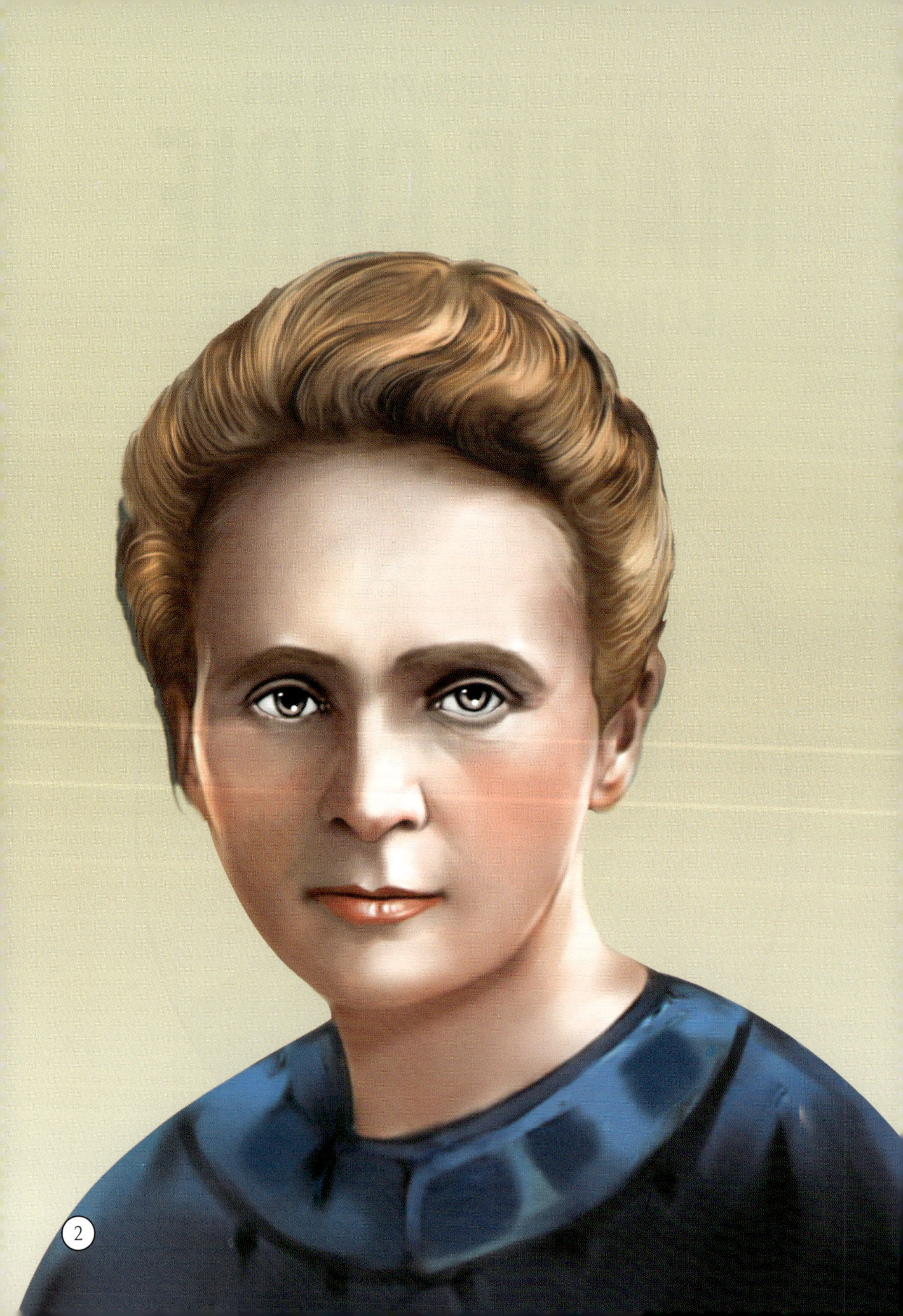

MARVELLOUS MARIE

Marie Salomea Skłodowska Curie was a Polish physicist and chemist. She is widely known for her research work in the field of radioactivity and for her discovery of the elements polonium and radium. She was awarded the Nobel Prize in the field of Physics in the year 1903, which she shared with Henri Becquerel, and her husband, Pierre Curie. She received her second Nobel Prize for Chemistry, in the year 1911. She is the first person and also the first woman to win the Nobel Prize into two different fields. She is also the first woman professor appointed at the University of Paris.

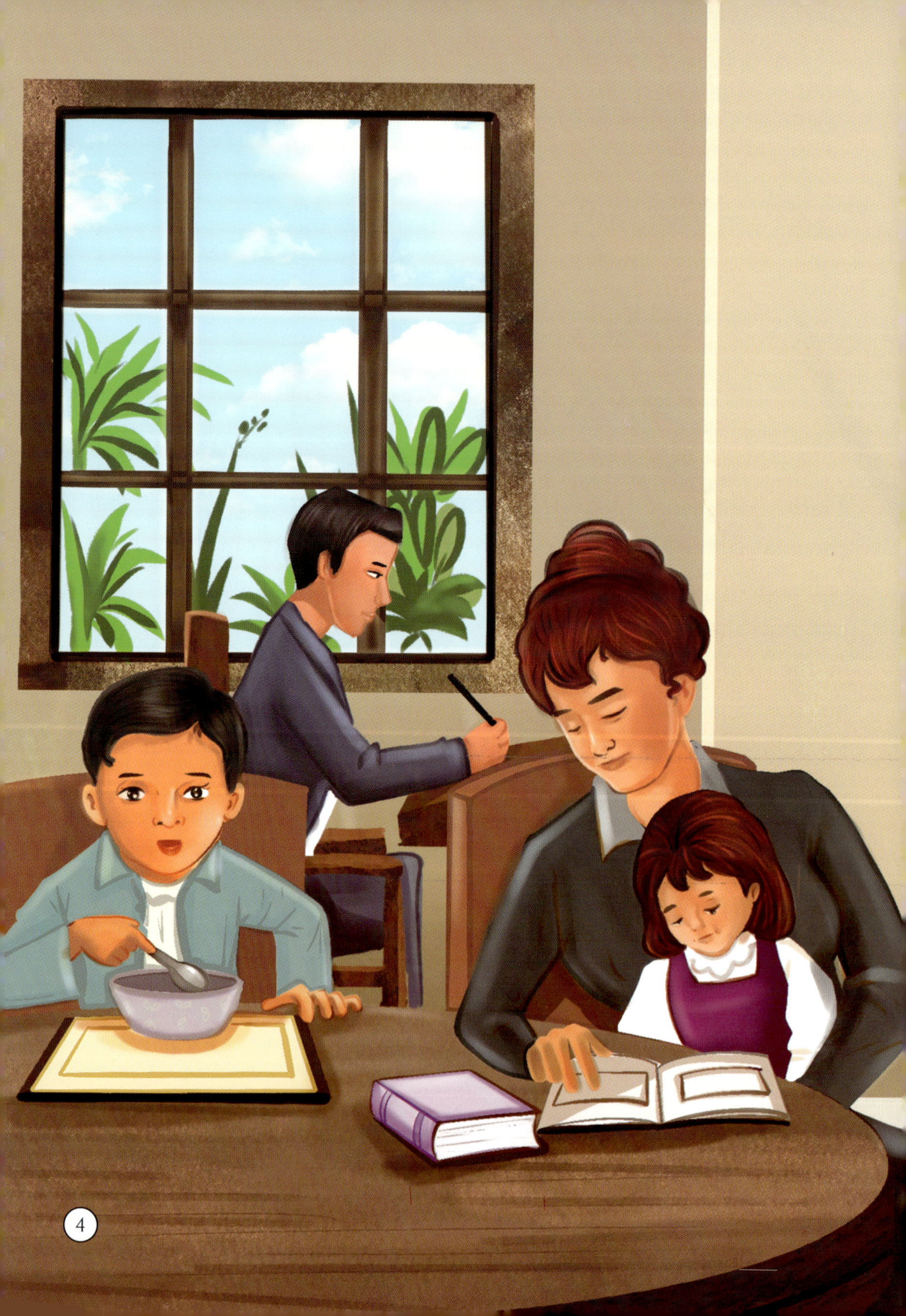

HUMBLE BEGINNINGS

Marie Curie was born on 7 November 1867, in Warsaw, Poland, which was then a part of the Russian Empire. She was the youngest in the family and had three elder sisters and a brother. Both her parents were secondary school teachers, who worked hard to make the ends meet. On both the maternal and paternal sides, the family had lost all the fortune and property in patriotic involvement, during the Polish national uprisings. This event had a significant impact on the economic condition of the family, and was the reason behind the life of struggles and hardships of Curie children.

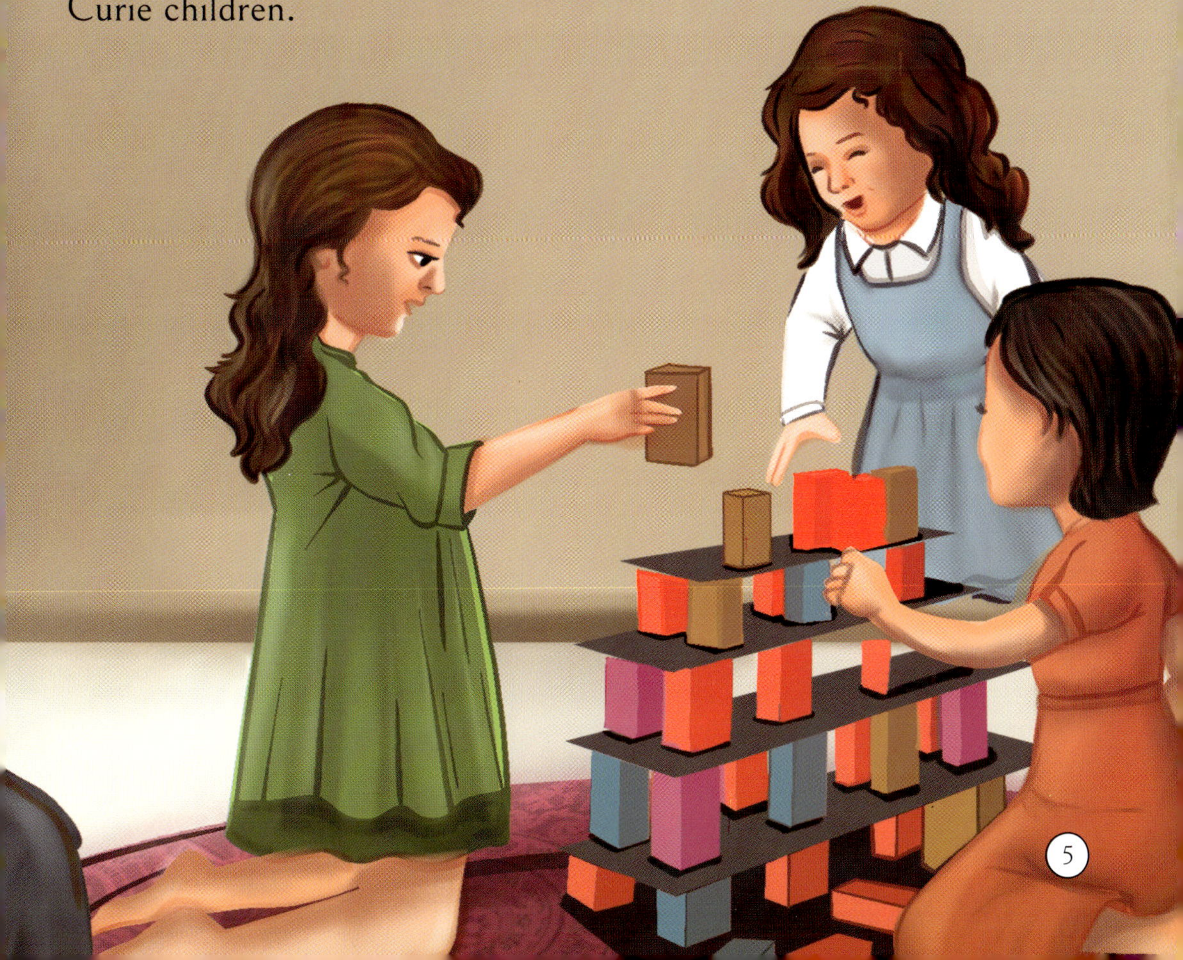

TRIALS AND TRIBULATIONS

Her father Władysław Skłodowski, was a teacher of mathematics and physics, so when Russian authorities prohibited laboratory instructions from Polish schools, he brought the scientific equipments home. This helped in laying the strong foundation for Mary's interest in the field of research.

Her father lost his job when the Russian authorities fired him for his pro-Polish sentiments, which forced him to take low-paying jobs. The family suffered huge

monetary losses due to bad investments thus, they lodged boys in their house as a measure to supplement their income.

At a very young age, Marie lost her eldest sibling, Zofia and three years later, in 1878, she lost her mother to tuberculosis.

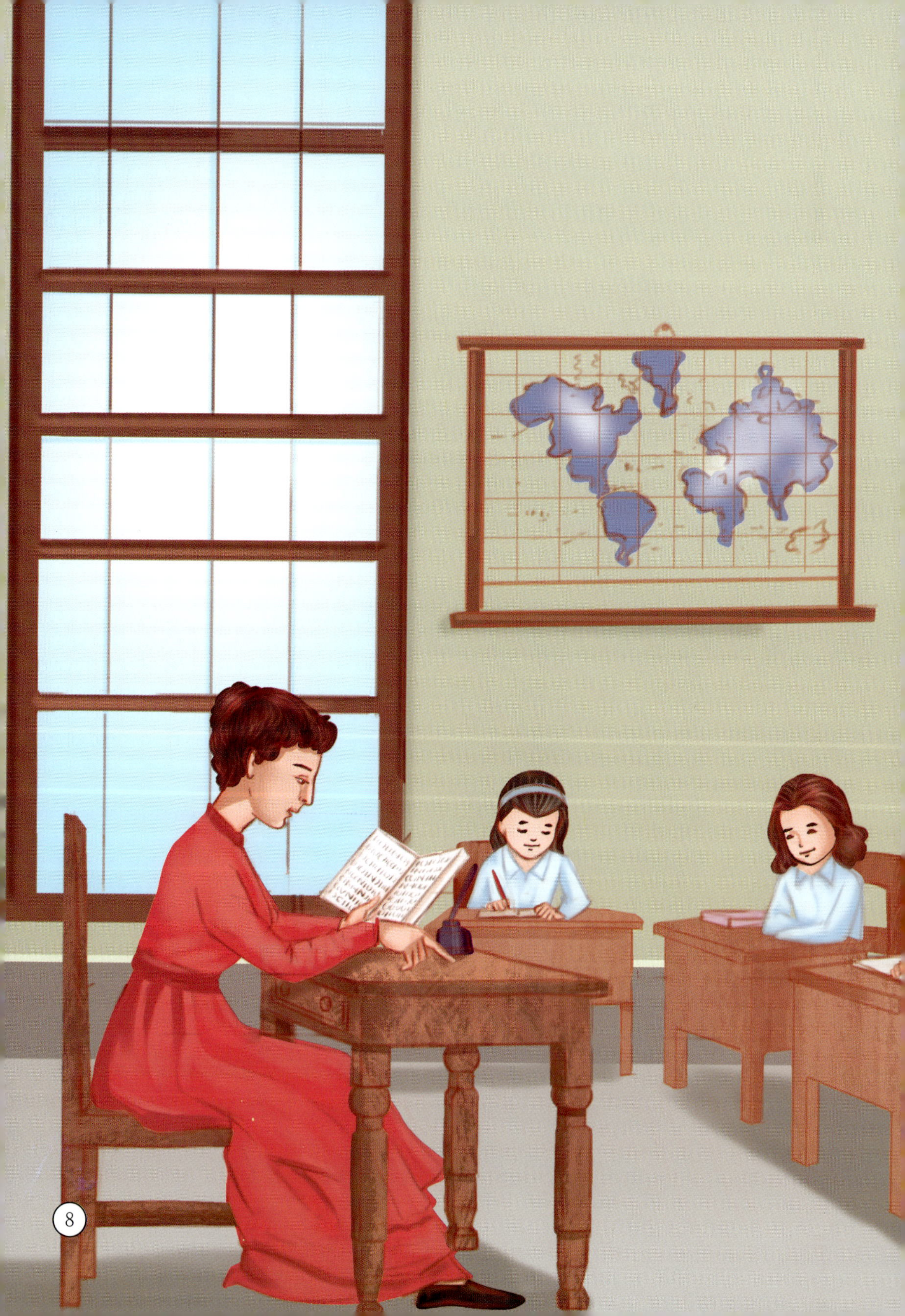

SISTER'S PROMISE

Marie joined a boarding school after her mother's demise and later attended a gymnasium for girls, from which she graduated with a gold medal. She was a prodigious child who was blessed with a remarkable memory and immense talent. After completing her secondary education, she couldn't enroll for higher studies due to the lack of funds. She and her sister Bronisława, attended the clandestine Flying University, a set of underground educational institutes that educated young women for higher studies.

Marie made an agreement with her sister Bronisława, that she would support her with financial assistance, for the completion of her medical studies in Paris. In return, she also had to provide similar assistance to her. In order to fulfill the promise made to her sister, Marie took a job as a governess and tutored young kids. She utilized her spare time in advancing her knowledge by studying physics, mathematics and chemistry.

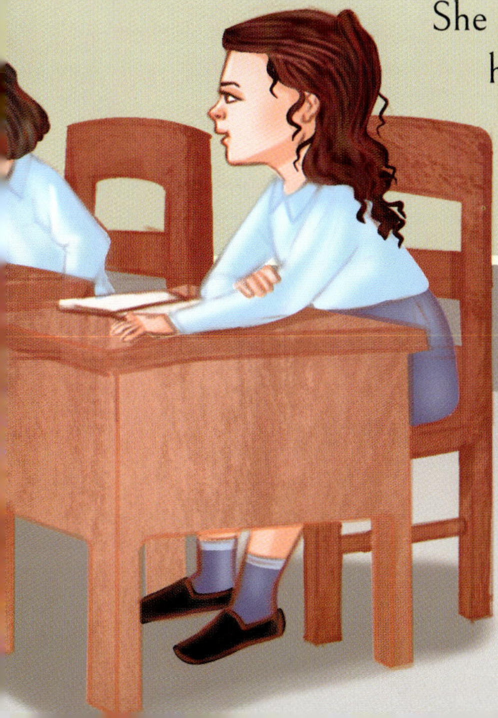

UNBOWED, UNBENT & UNBROKEN

In 1890, Bronisława called Marie to Paris but she declined the offer saying she cannot afford the university fee and needed a few more years to arrange for the necessary funds. But this time her father came to her rescue and supplemented her with monetary help.

Thus, in 1891, Marie made her way to Paris and enrolled herself in Sorbonne. Upon entering the university, she dedicated herself completely to her studies. She sustained on her meager savings and survived the bitter cold of Paris by wearing all the clothing she possessed. Her dedication was such, she used to study for hours and hours, sometimes even forgetting to eat or drink. She led a difficult life in Paris, she tutored during the day and studied at night.

Despite the circumstances, she finished her master's degree in physics in 1893, and with some aid from her research fellowship, she finished her second degree in mathematics the following year.

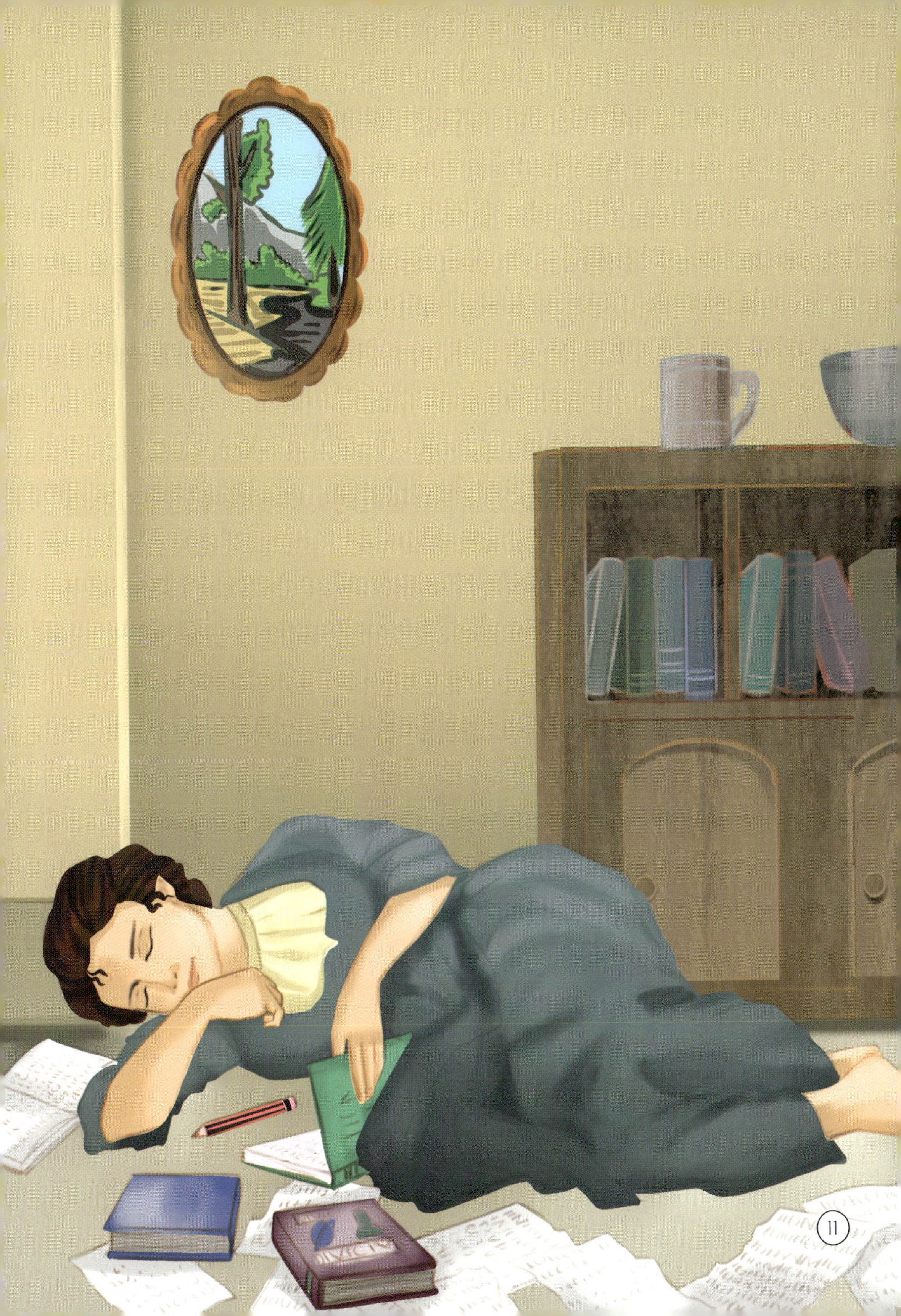

A NEW PARTNERSHIP

Marie started her scientific journey in Paris. After her graduation from Sorbonne, she was searching for a large laboratory to conduct her research work: the study of the magnetic properties of steel. This quest of hers brought her in acquaintance with Pierre Curie. They were introduced through a common friend. But it was their shared passion for science, that brought them together.

And soon this scientific partnership turned into a lifetime commitment. But this journey was not easy; when Pierre first proposed to Marie, she declined his offer saying, she was planning to go back to her native country. Thus, true to

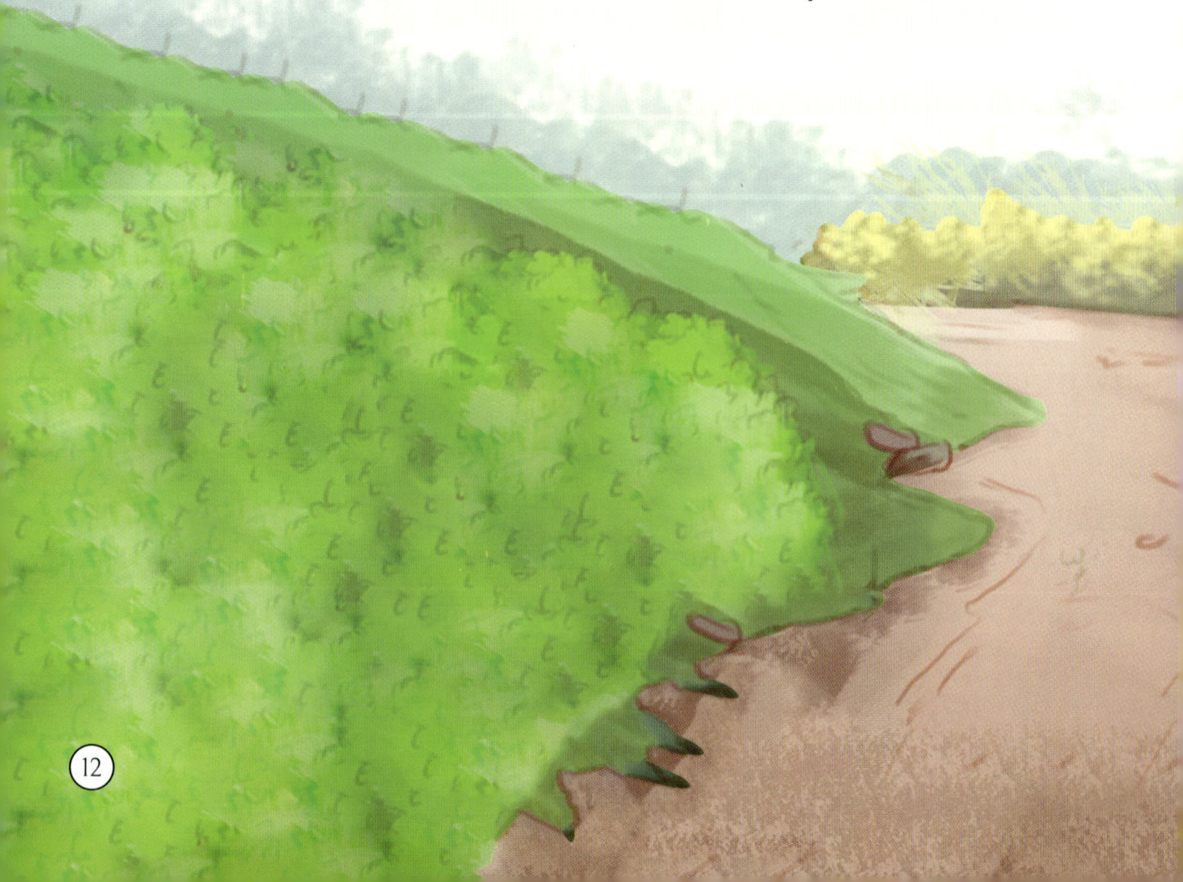

her words, in summer of 1894 she returned to Warsaw. Unfortunately, she was denied admission at Kraków University because of the rising sexism in academia.

The unfair circumstances forced her to return to Paris, where she pursued her Ph.D. and married Pierre on 26 July 1895.

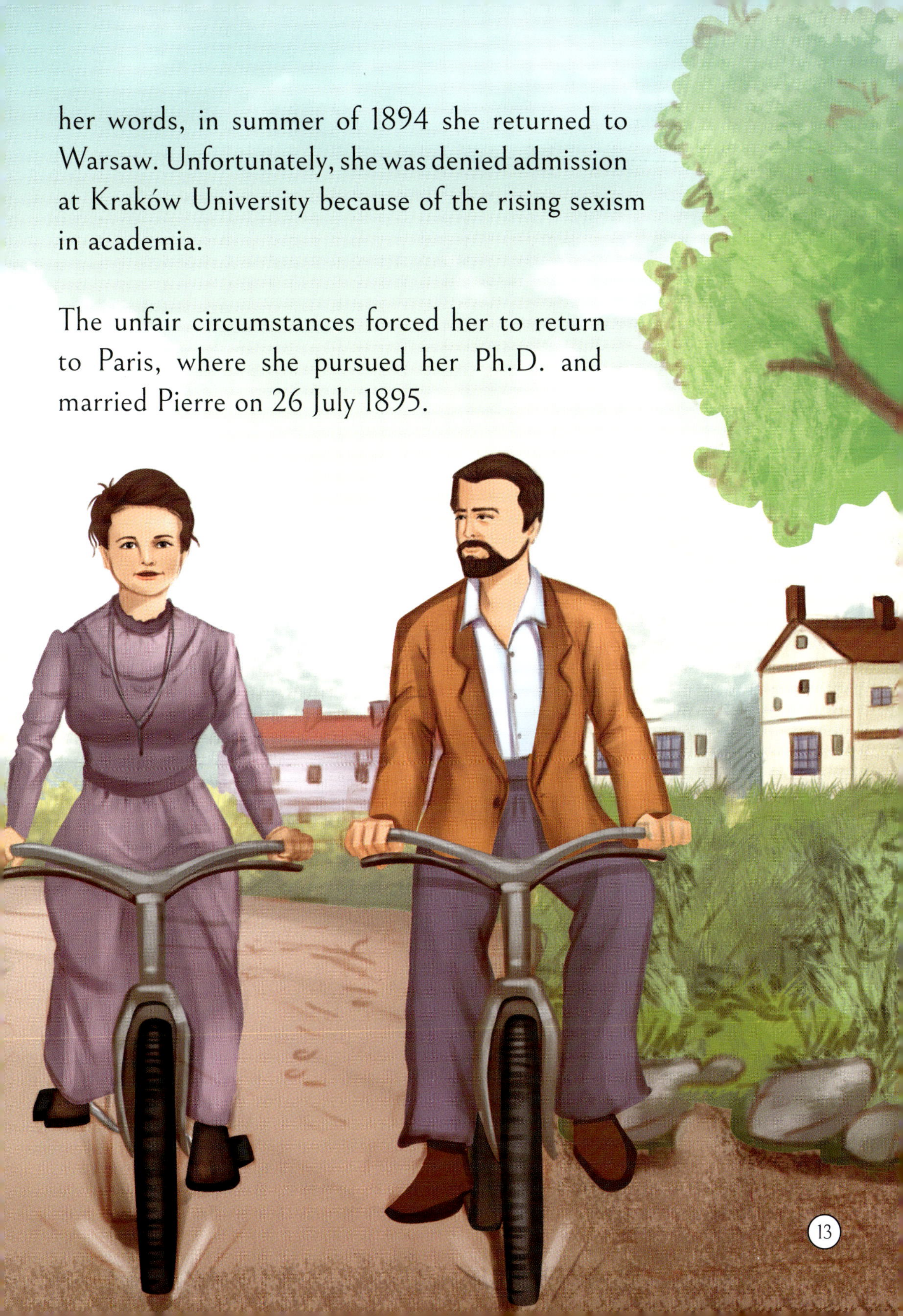

REVOLUTION IN SCIENCE

Henri Becquerel's discovery in 1896, proved that uranium salts emit rays that resemble x-rays. This sparked Curie's interest in the field. She decided to conduct her own experiments and discovered that uranium rays remained constant irrespective of the form of the sample. Thus, she theorized that this radiation was due to the atomic structure of the element and not due to the interaction of some molecules. This exemplary idea brought a revolution in the field of atomic physics by disproving the long-standing assumption that atoms are indivisible. Curie coined the term 'radioactivity' to describe this phenomenon.

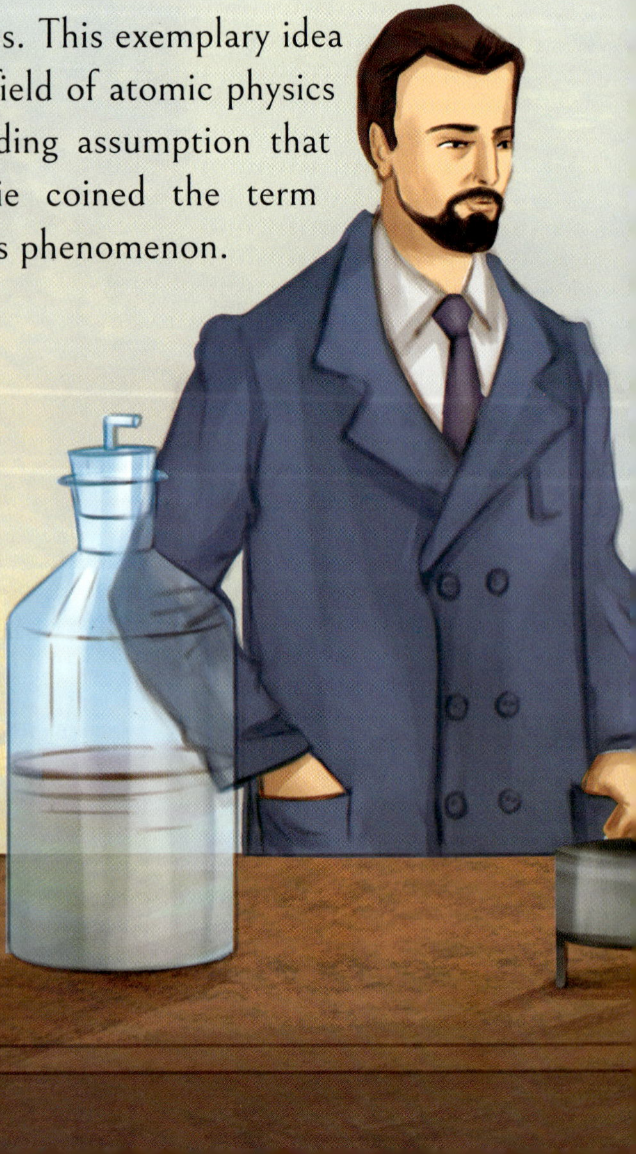

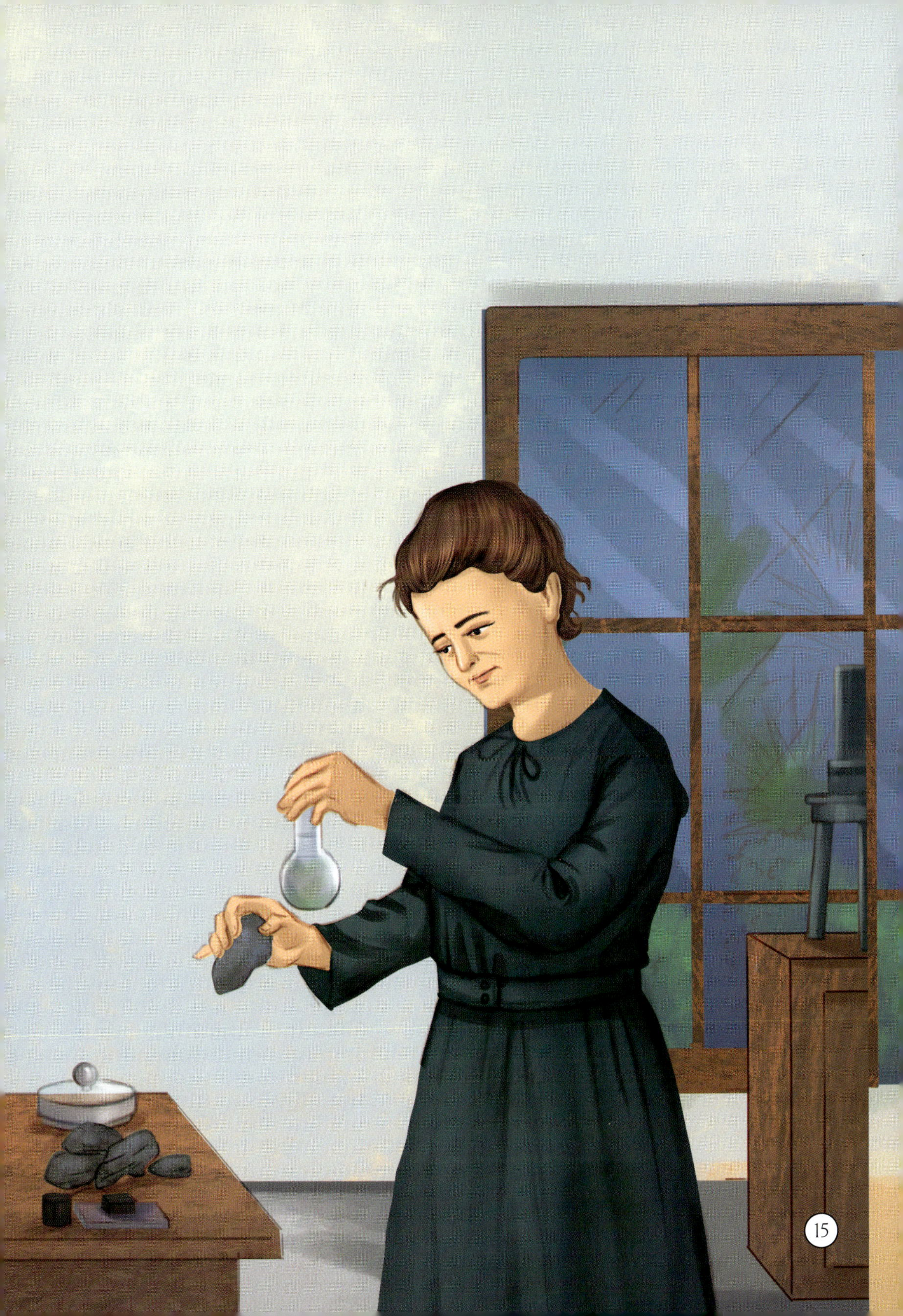

OBLIVIOUS

In 1897, Marie gave birth to her first daughter, Irène. During this time, along with her research work, she also took up teaching in order to support her family. During her teaching tenure, she introduced new methods of learning, based on experimental demonstrations.

However, both she and her husband were still looking for a suitable laboratory space to conduct their research work. For a long time, they used a converted shed of a medical school, formerly a dissecting room, as a laboratory.

This shed was neither waterproof nor it was properly ventilated. Curies continued with their research work in these challenging circumstances. They were not aware of the disastrous effects of radiation exposure; thus, they conducted their research unabatedly in this unprotected environment.

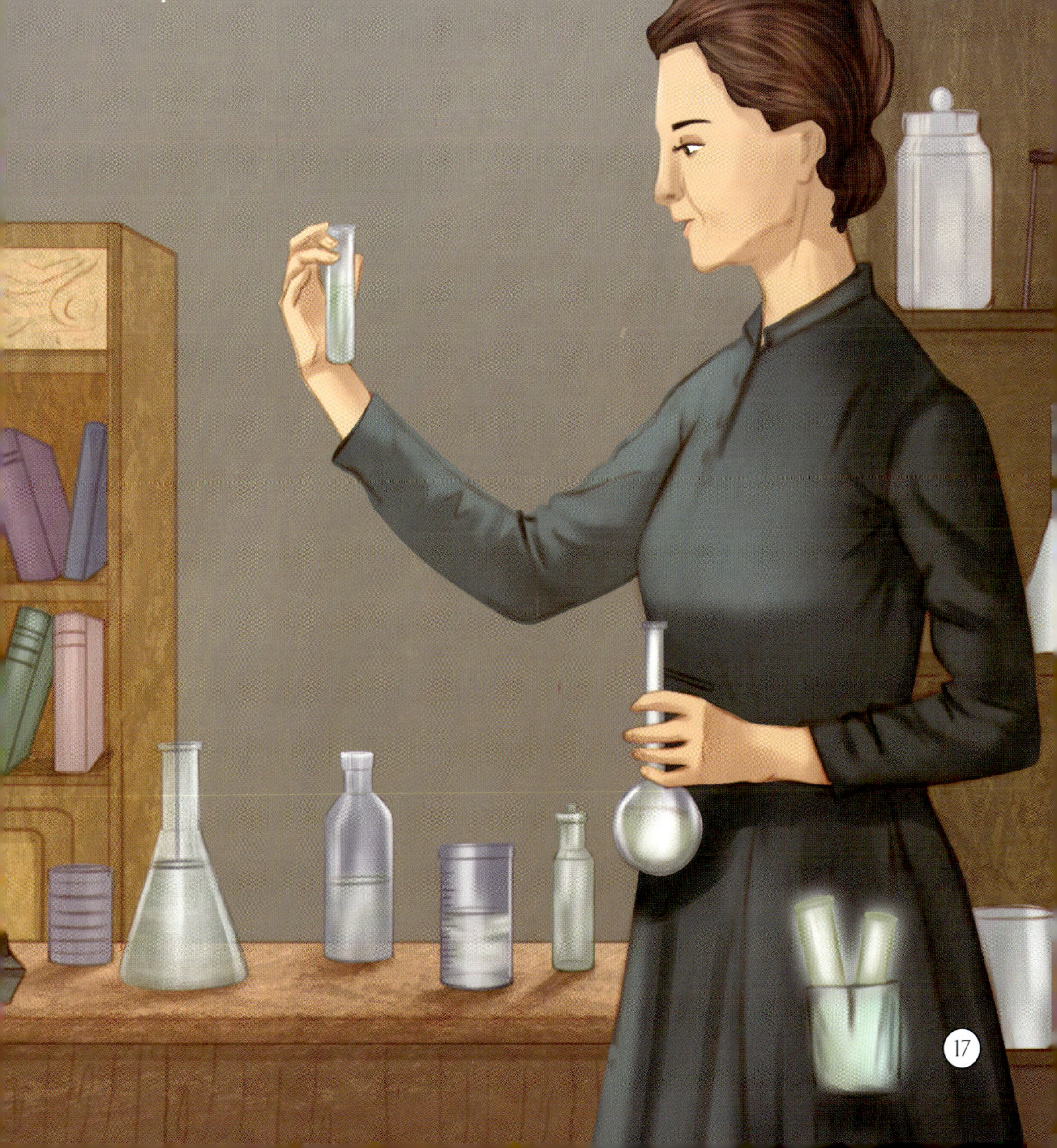

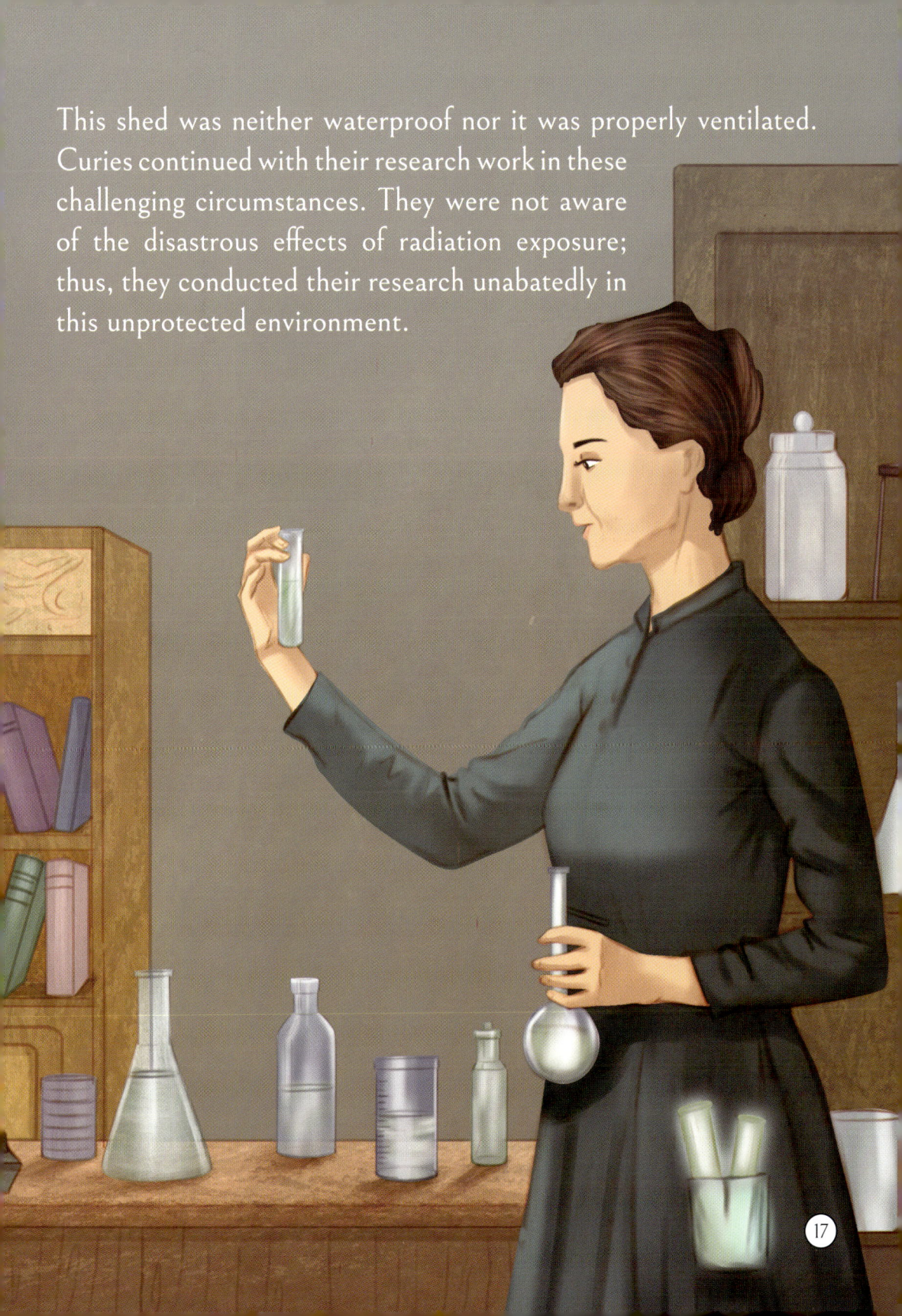

TRIUMPH OF SUCCESS

In 1903, the Royal Swedish Academy of Sciences awarded Nobel Prize for Physics to Marie Curie, Pierre Curie and Henri Becquerel for their outstanding contribution in the understanding of radiation phenomena. Being shy in nature, the couple decided against attending the ceremony in person but later relented to the idea.

The prize money opened a door of opportunities for the Curies. On one hand, the University of Paris offered professorship to Pierre Curie, along with the chairmanship of the physics department. On the other, the money allowed them to employ a laboratory assistant, allowing them the necessary aid, for their laborious research work.

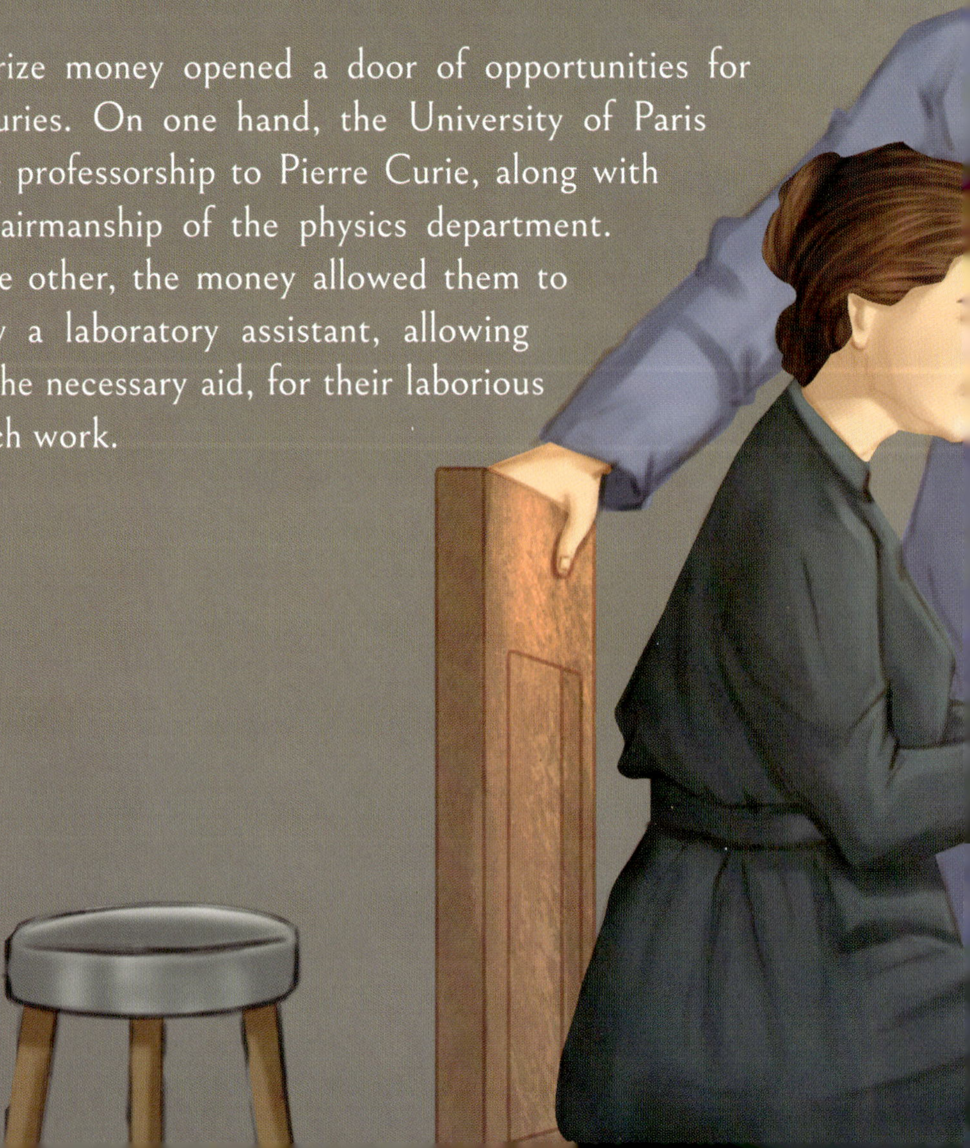

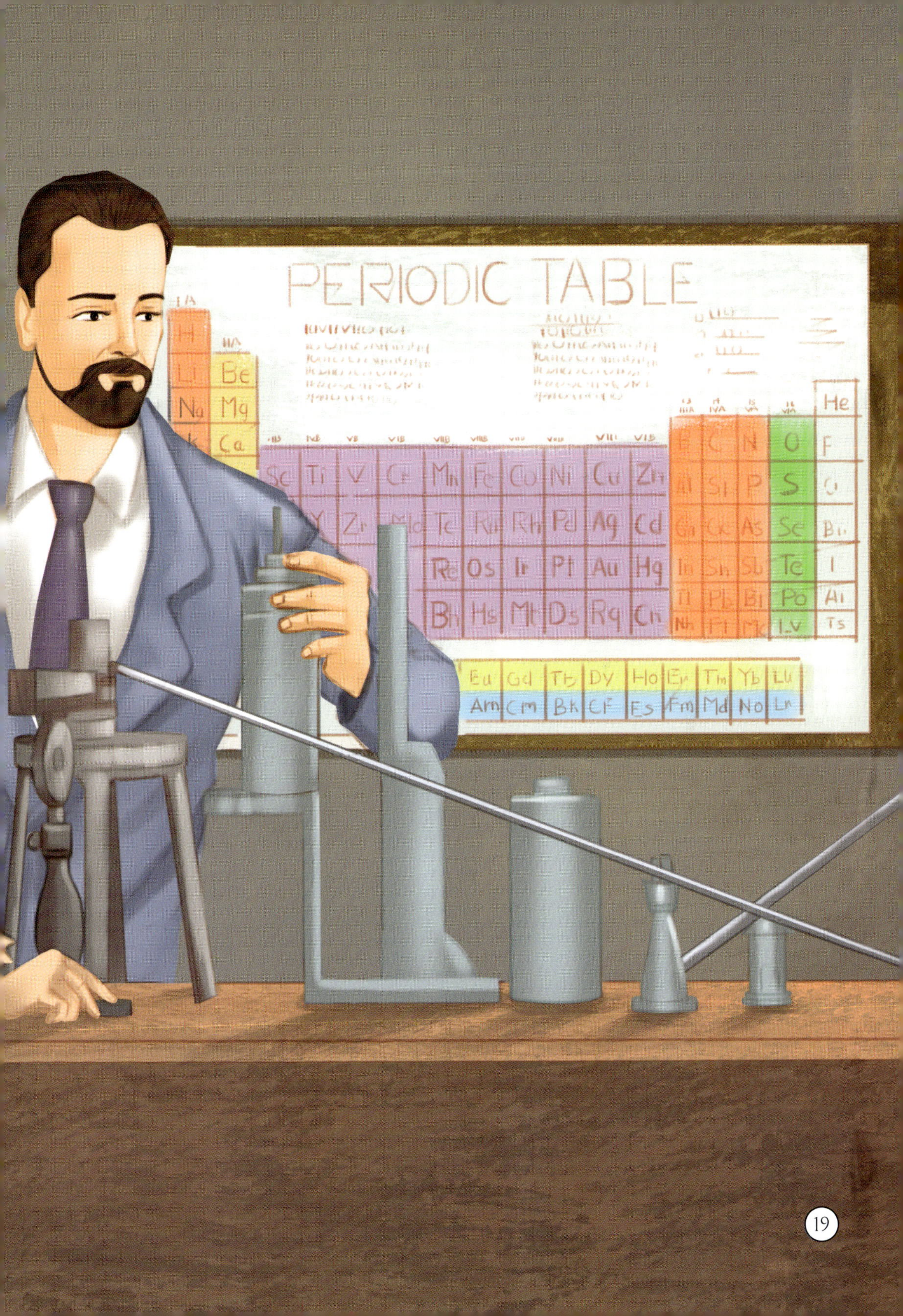
PERIODIC TABLE

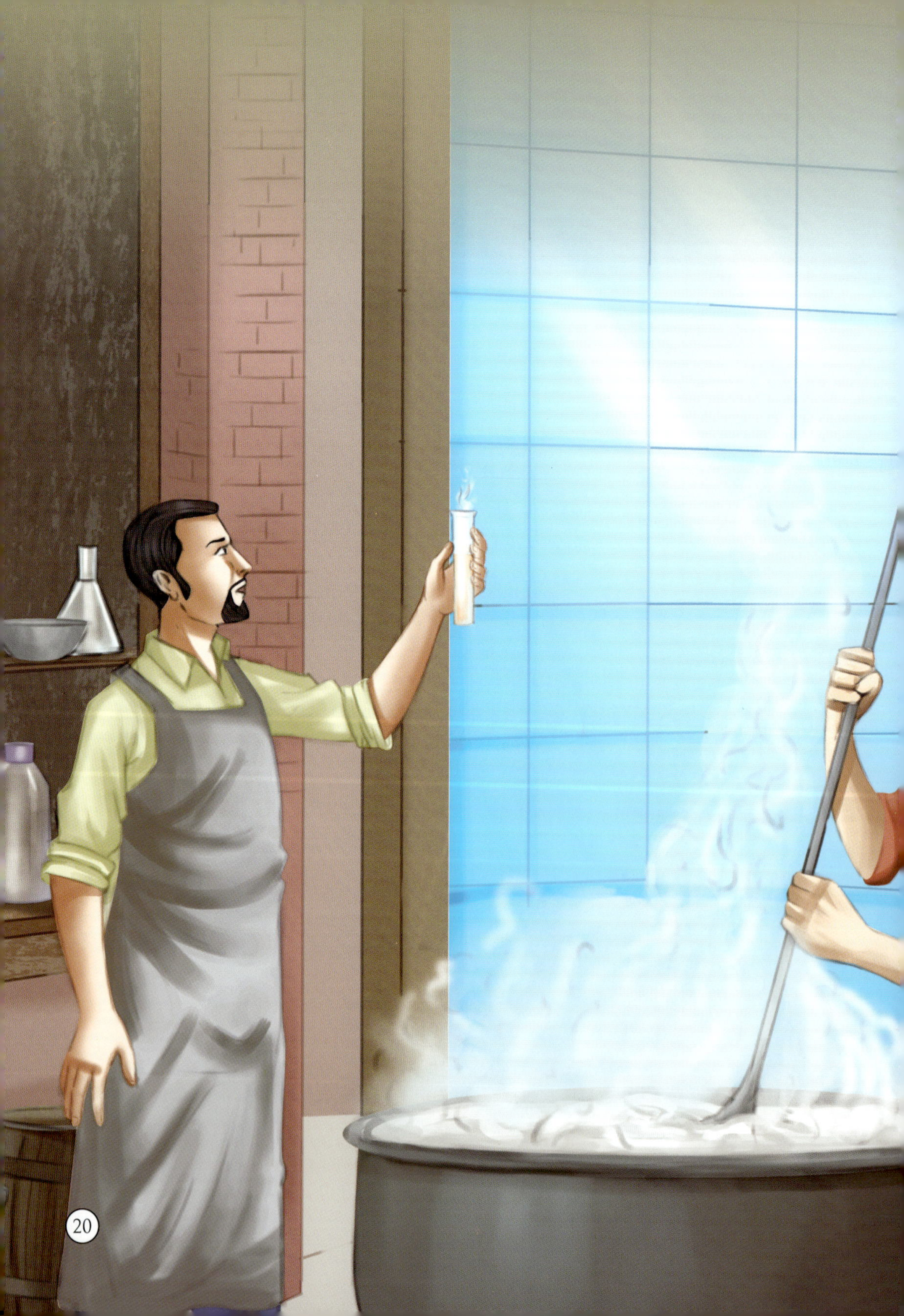

NEW DISCOVERIES

While conducting her research, Marie came across the samples of a mineral called pitchblende, containing the ore of uranium. She observed that pitchblende was highly radioactive even after the extraction of uranium from it. This convinced Marie that there was something more to the mineral.

Both Pierre and Marie Curie set out to search for this new element. They devised a plan for separating the pitchblende into chemical components. They worked day and night, stirring the large cauldrons with iron rods. Eventually, they extracted a 330 times more radioactive element than uranium and named it, polonium, after her native country Poland.

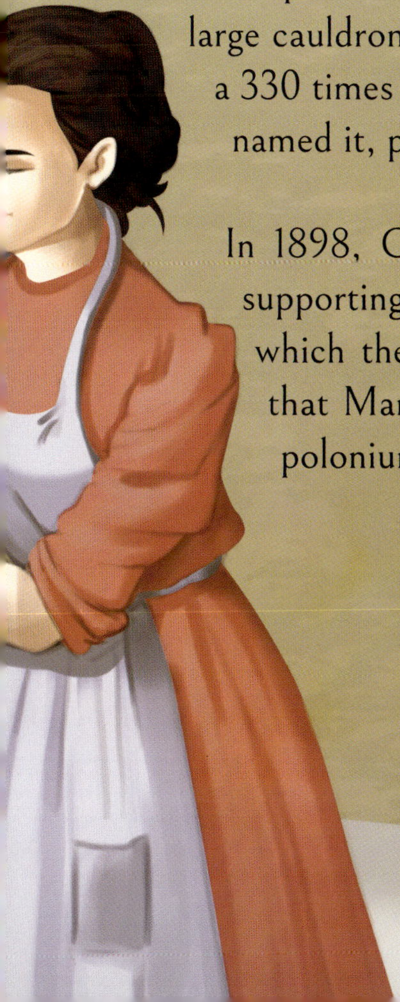

In 1898, Curies published strong pieces of evidence supporting the discovery of a new radioactive element which they called radium. But it was only in 1902, that Marie was finally able to extract pure forms of polonium and radium.

WHEN TRAGEDY STRUCK

In 1904, Marie Curie gave birth to her second daughter, Ève. She was a true polish at heart and wanted her children to be aware of the culture and place from which their mother came from. She hired a polish governess to teach her daughters, her native language and even took them to visit Poland.

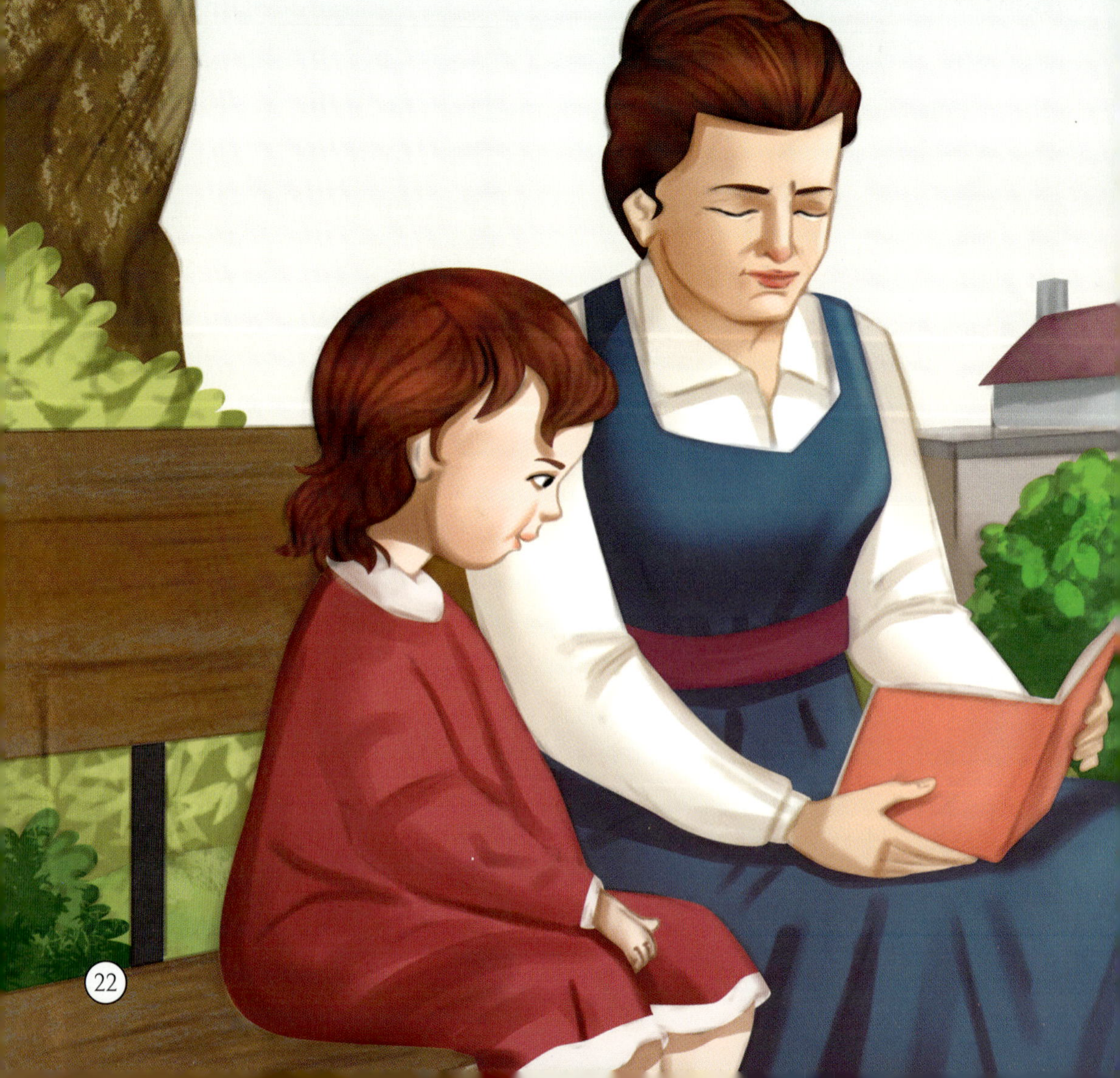

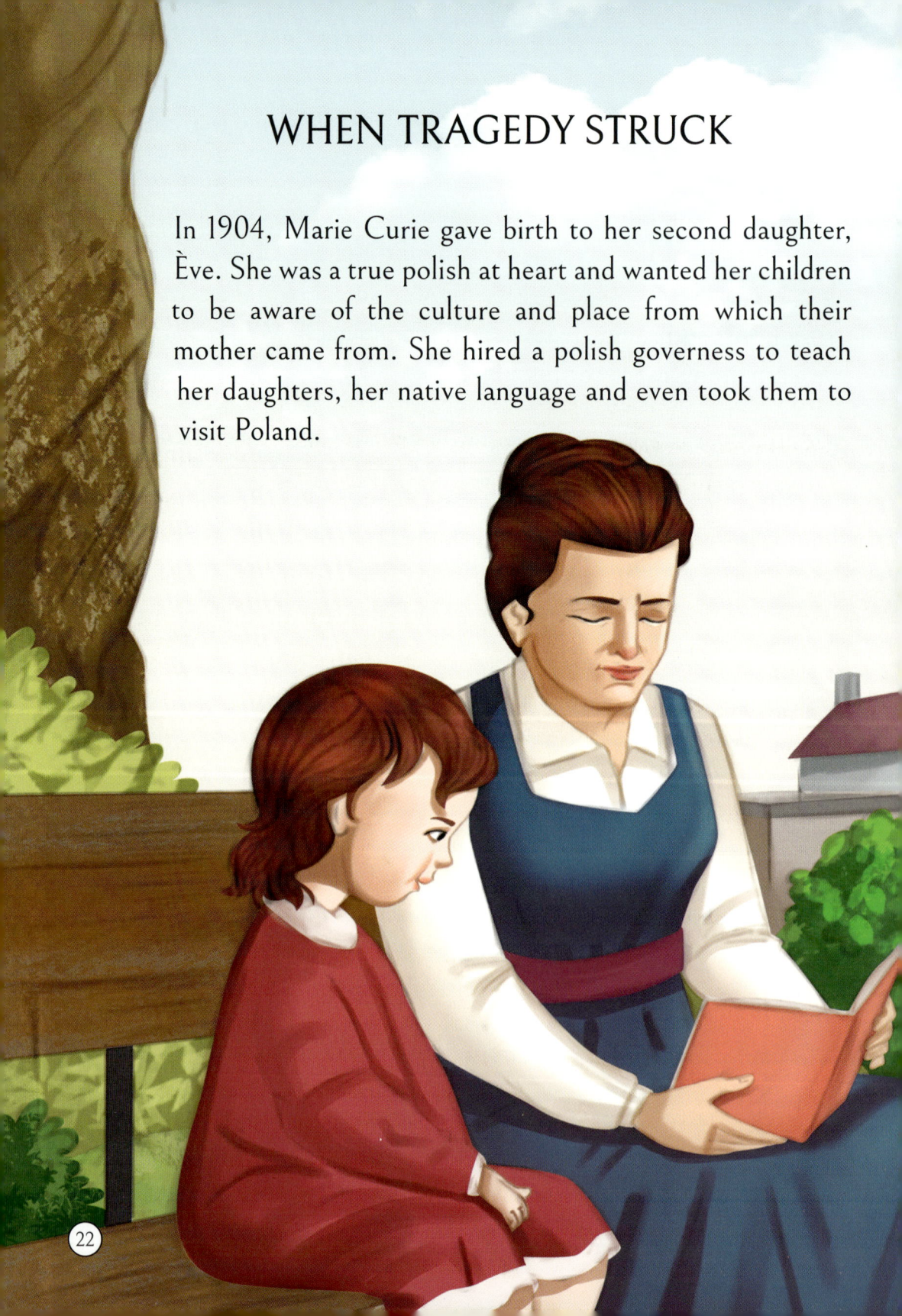

After receiving the Nobel Prize and securing her doctorate in 1903, life was happy and falling into place until tragedy struck in 1906.

Her husband Pierre Curie, died in a road accident, after being knocked down by a horse-driven cart. This incident had a significant impact on her, but despite the hardships and misfortunes that life threw upon her, she stood up and kept on working towards her dreams. She went on to succeed her husband's chair and became the first woman to become a professor at the University of Paris.

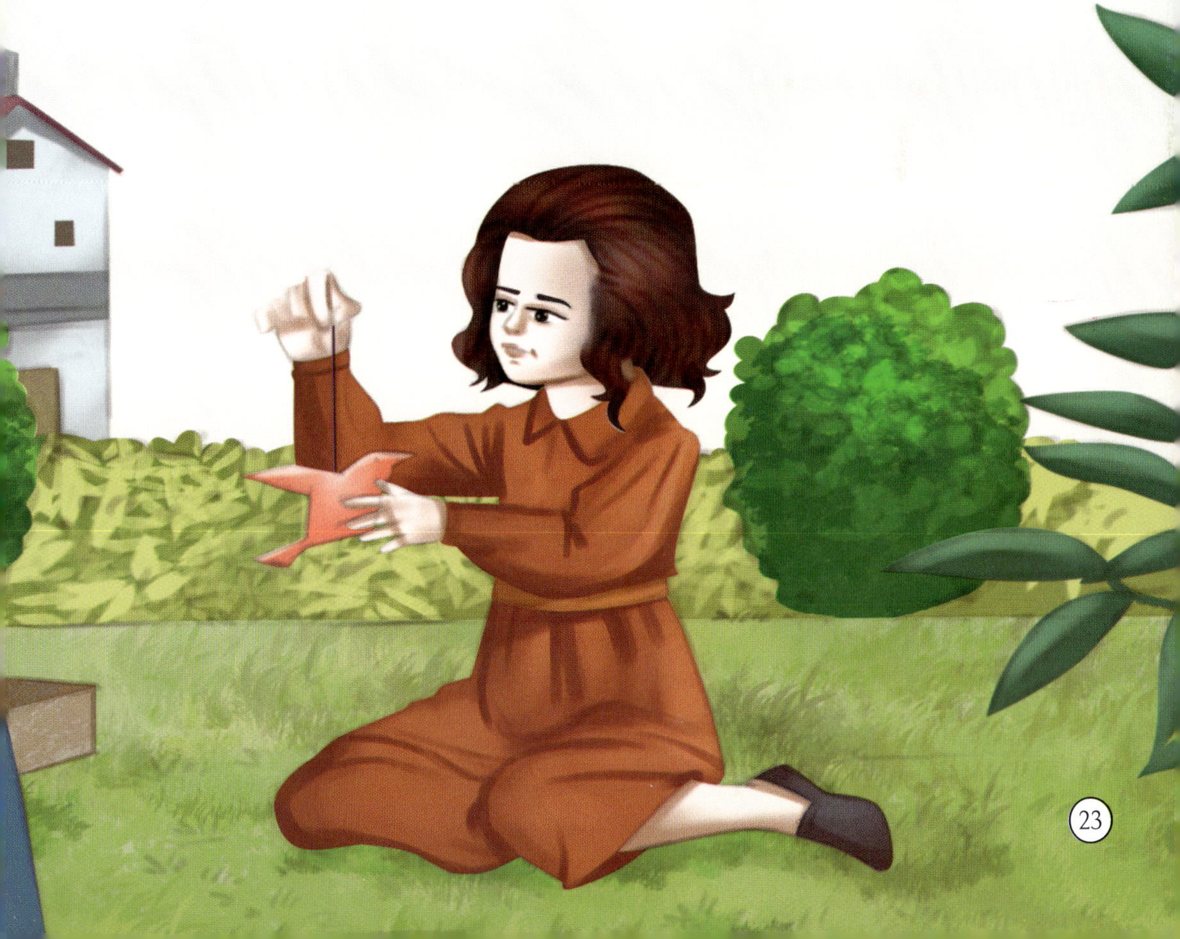

YOUR DREAMS ARE MINE

After the bitter loss of her husband, Curie directed all her energy towards her work. She decided to make a world-class laboratory, in order to pay tribute to her late husband. In 1910, her fundamental treatise on radioactivity was published. In the following year, she received her second Nobel Prize for Chemistry, for the isolation of pure radium.

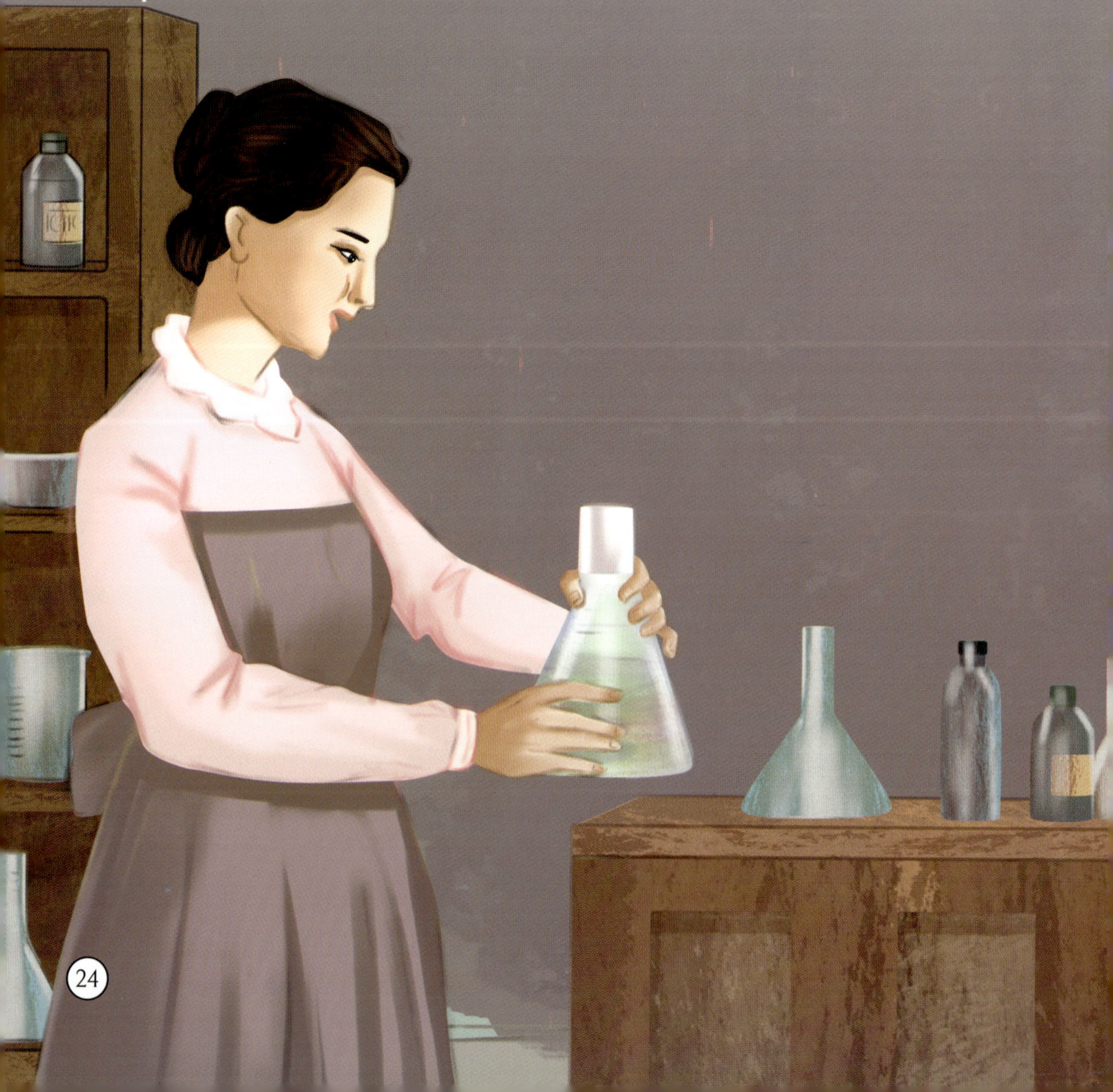

In 1914, she succeeded in fulfilling her long-standing dream of a world-class laboratory, which found its shape in the form of the Radium Institute at the University of Paris. Sorbonne built two laboratories in the Radium Institute, one for the study of radioactivity under Marie Curie's direction and the other, for biological research for the treatment of cancer.

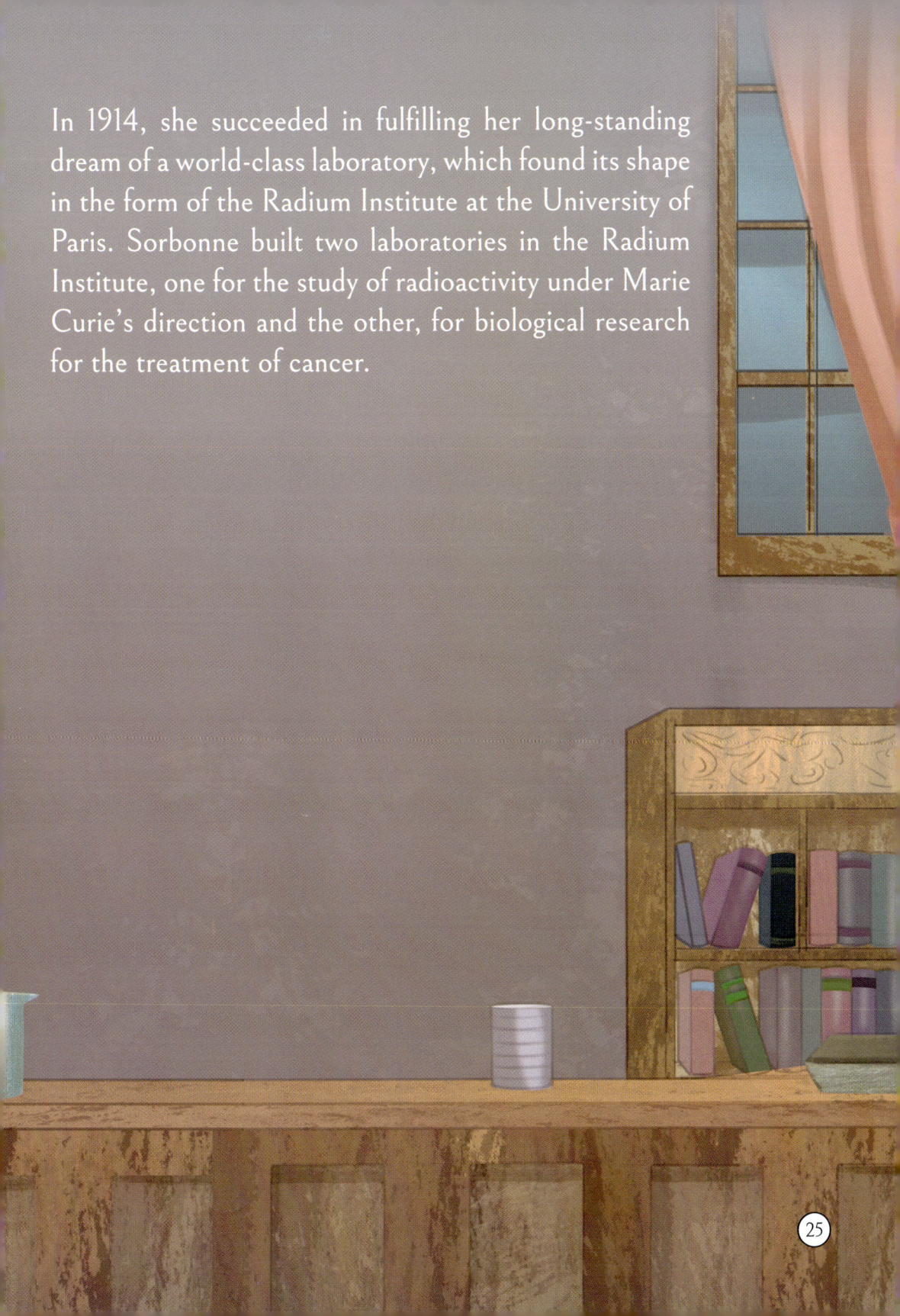

STANDING TOGETHER

During the First World War, Marie developed small, mobile X-ray units. These radiography units were popularly called as petites Curies or 'Little Curies'.

With the help of her daughter Irène, then aged 17, she treated over a million soldiers using X-ray units. These units were deployed at the casualty clearing station, near the front line, to assist the battlefield surgeons. She used her X-ray units to aid wounded soldiers, in order to locate fractures, bullets or any other internal injuries.

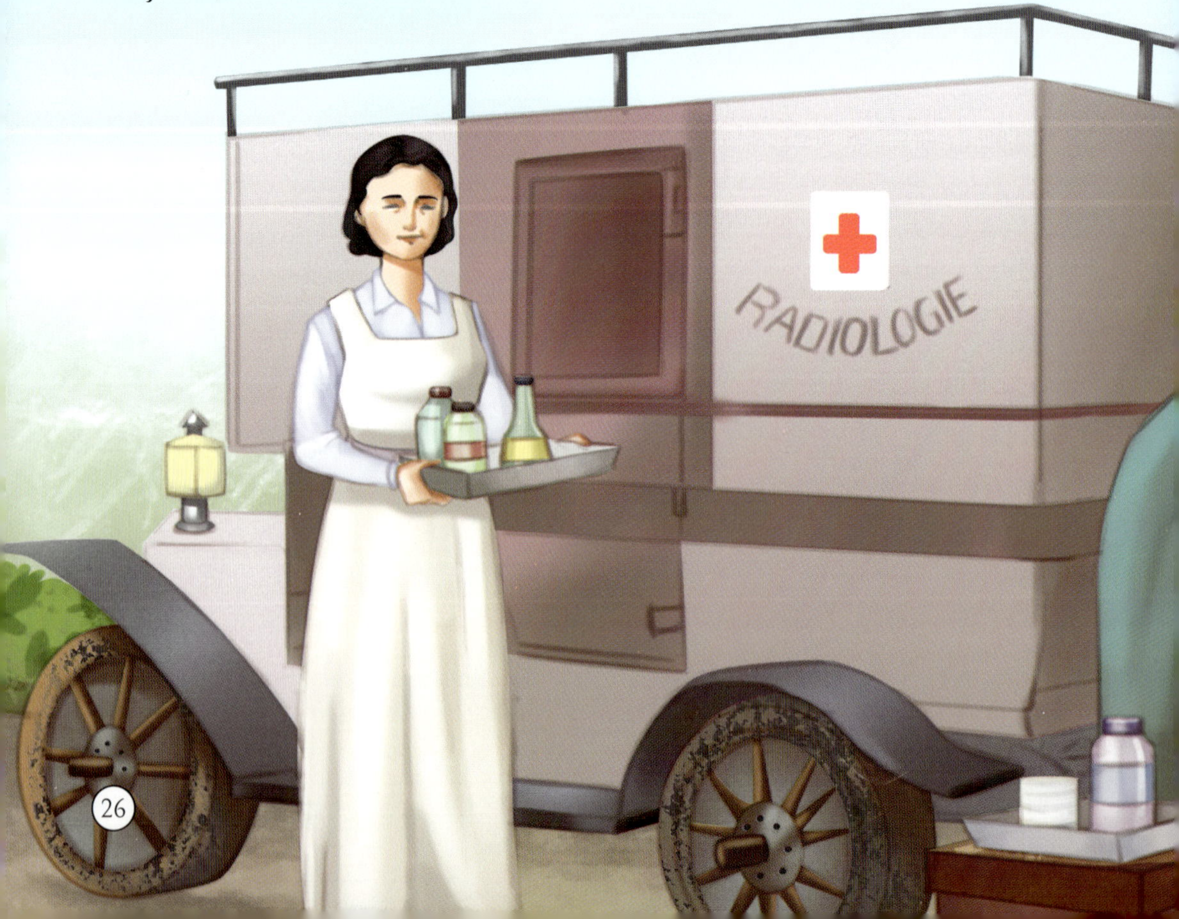
RADIOLOGIE

In 1914, she became the director of the Red Cross Radiological Service and was a pioneer in setting up France's first military radiology center. During this time, she also toured Paris for collecting money, vehicles and supplies for the aid of war soldiers.

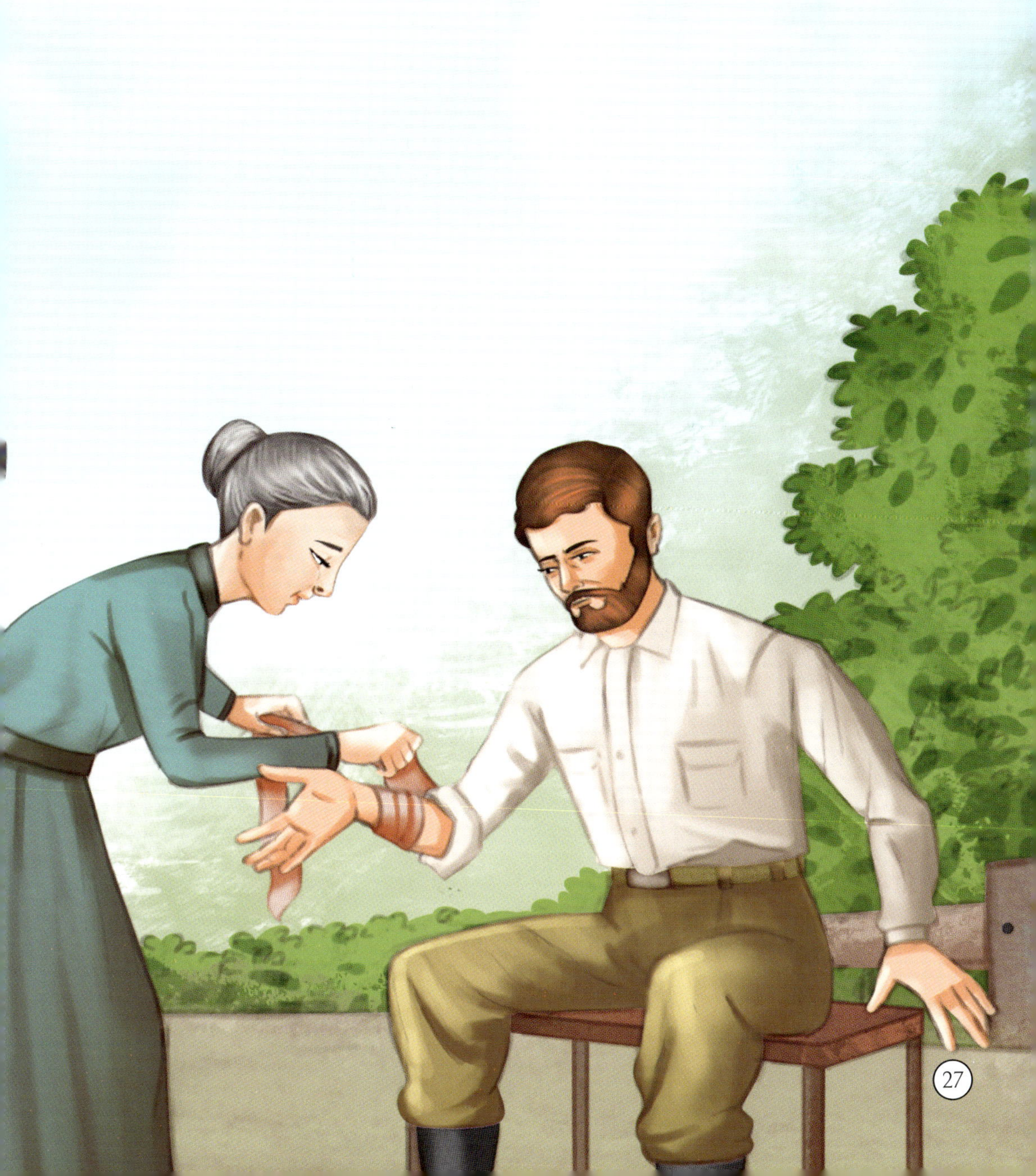

AT THE END OF THE ROAD

Marie Curie died on 4 July 1934, at the age of 66, after suffering from aplastic anemia. During her research, the damaging effects of radiation exposure were not known. Thus, her long-time exposure to radiation without any safety measures had a damaging effect on her bone marrow. She carried test tubes containing radioactive substances in her pockets and also stored them in her desk drawers.

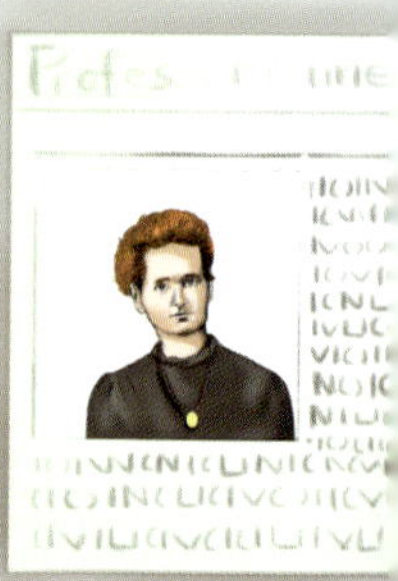

In 1995, Marie and Pierre Curie's remains were moved to Panthéon, the French National Mausoleum, in Paris. She became the first woman to receive such honor based on her own achievements. Her office and laboratory are preserved under the aegis of the Curie Museum in the Curie pavilion of the Radium Institute.

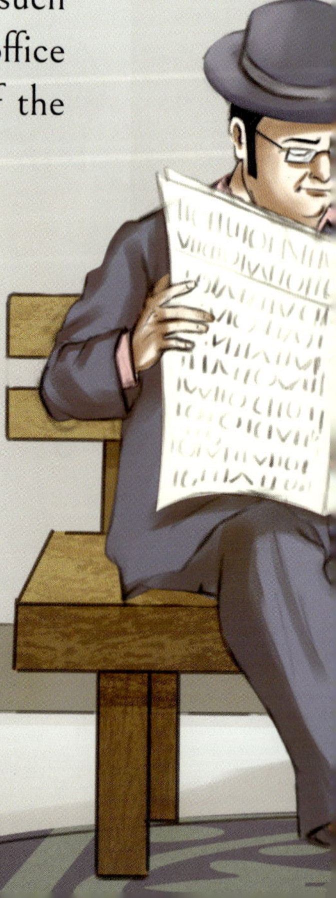

Carrying the Curie legacy forward, her daughter Irène Joliot-Curie along with her husband, Frédéric Joliot-Curie won Nobel Prize in Chemistry in 1935, for their research work on the synthesis of new radioactive elements, making the total Nobel Prize tally of Curies to five.

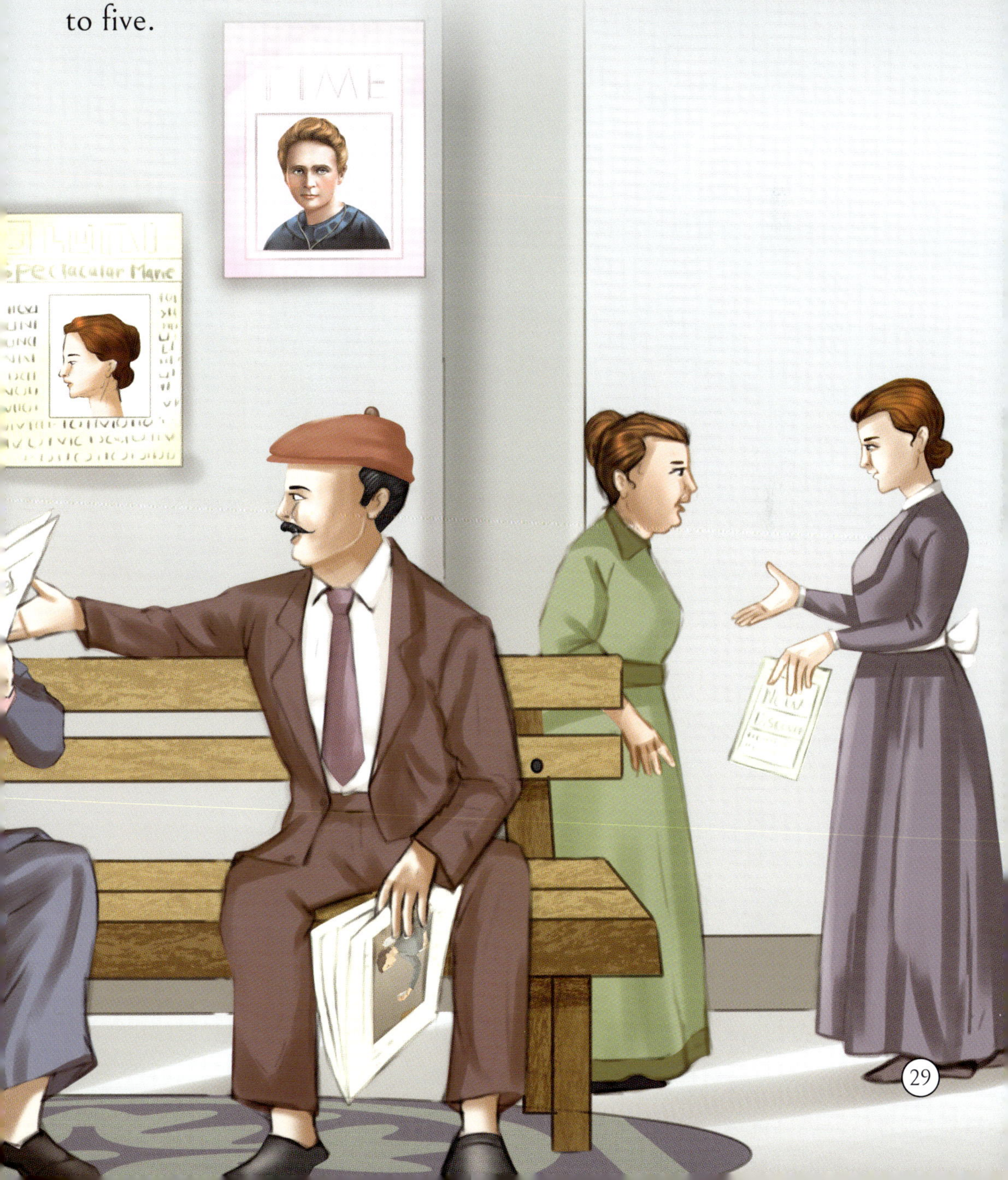
TIME

AN EVER-LASTING LEGACY

Marie Curie is an inspiration to the world, her unprecedented achievements as a scientist left an indelible mark on the world.

Her undaunted strength, uncommon intensity and remarkable confidence helped her touch the sky of success and taught the world that with one's unflinching determination one can make their own way into the world, unscathed by the demanding circumstances that come along the way.

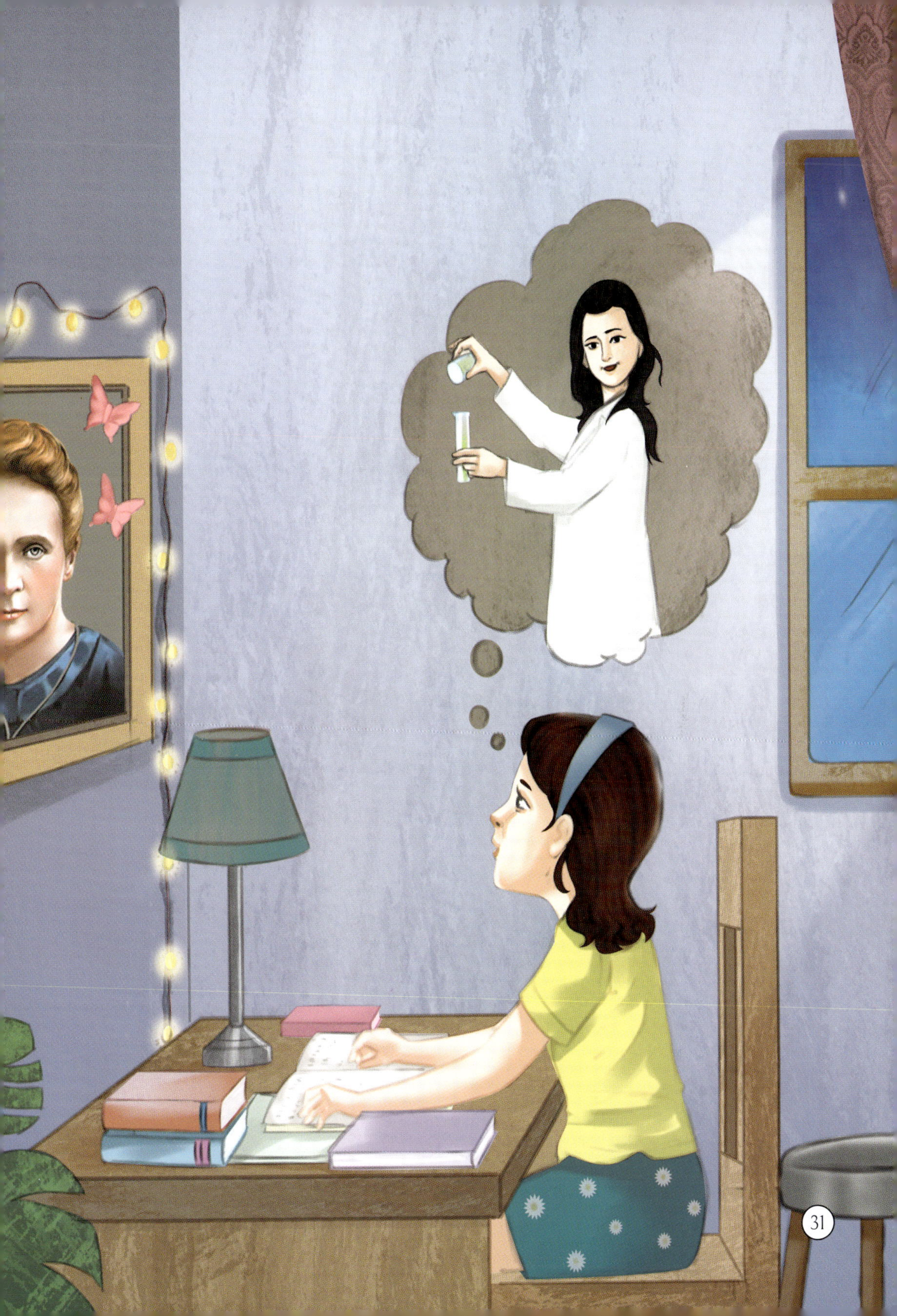

1867 : Marie Curie is born in Warsaw, Poland

1891 : Moves to Paris to study at Sorbonne

1895 : Marries physicist Pierre Curie

1897 : Gives birth to her first daughter, Irène

1902 : Marie Curie works with radium

1903 : Nobel Prize in Physics with her husband, Pierre Curie, and Henri Becquerel

1904 : Gives birth to her second daughter, Ève; Pierre Curie begins teaching at Sorbonne

1906 : Death of Pierre Curie; Marie assumes her husband's position at Sorbonne, becoming the first female professor of the university

1911 : Second Nobel Prize in Chemistry

1914 : Develops X-rays

1934 : Marie Curie dies